Down the Grassy Aisles

Down the Grassy Aisles

Poems by

Aruna Gurumurthy

Cover design by Shay Culligan

ISBN: 978-1-952326-06-6

Kelsay Books
502 South 1040 East, A-119
American Fork, Utah, 84003

For my world

my mom, Viji *ma;*
my husband, my love, Vijay;
my dazzling daughter, Diya

❦

Acknowledgments

My sincere acknowledgments to Lisa Joy Tomey, and Cindy Hochman (of "100 Proof" Copyediting Services) for being extraordinary proofreaders and copy editors.

To my poet friends, Sylvia Freeman, Jeanne Julian, Alta Dawson, Patricia Killian Deaton, Judy Goodenough, Ed Lyons, and Aarti Sanan who helped with sewing some of my poems together. This work wouldn't have been possible without your support.

Many thanks to the publications that brought these poems to the world, some in slightly different versions

First Literary Review: "The Downpour"

DIYA, A Megawatt Approach to Change: "Unique Ambitions"

A Beginning to the End: "Up in the Air"

A Beginning to the End: "Musings"

I can't thank enough the crazy dream I had one night that inspired me to write poems for peace and posterity.

Books by Aruna Gurumurthy

DIYA: A Megawatt Approach to Change

Spark: Poetic Creations

A Beginning to the End: A Poetic Journey

Buddha In the Brain

Puppet Dolls

Simplicity Beckons

Contents

Poetry at the Port

One Sunday in the December weeks of spring, we gather like geese at the pond. We gather at our port, amidst the charm in stacked hay, green splendor swaying, drooping from the sky. We listen and soak in poems as the rain soaks us in merry glory. My voice, still and sanguine, sings of the pigeons, the Ponte Vecchio crumbling from the laughter of lovers passing by, my mental piano going *allegro* for a thousand miles. Gladly, I am interrupted by the knocks of my five-going-on-six little charmer and the sighs of the spectators, as though gently moving the unseen curtains. Shall I say simplicity beckons?

The Embrace

The growing vine, she helixes around the naked branches of the Oak. She travels through a gazebo, she dances about, the bounce loosening up a passerby's grimace, with a musical glow, an *oomph* to the soul. Resplendent raw sienna, her body touches the tree. A cherub of twenty-four months, she has grown and crawls to embrace me. A subtle Shangri-La, a mystic Bethlehem, the dancing duos in the arms of Mother Earth.

Those Were the Rainy Days

Summer knocks, then beckons. I remember the beats of the Bombay monsoons. Downpours slapping us with life. The raindrops descend on my glossy pink raincoat-covered body, then into my warm soul. Colas and popsicles wetting a mouthful. A reason for the water balloons to fill and toss at tiny shirts in an ongoing bonanza of thrill. A display of amusement. Squeezing every bit of enthusiasm into a tiny umbrella, swinging arms like Maria in *The Sound of Music,* singing "rain, rain, go away," drenched and dancing to eternity. In the downpour, we devour corn from the neighbor's corn stand. He roasts the corn, rubs red cayenne and crushed peppercorns and drizzles it with lemon drops, tasting like butter had bestowed its best on us. Our hearts trip into fields of love, tickled tongues licking the peripheral remains of the snack inside our cutesy cheeks. *Aahaa,* is this life, or is this love? Those are the Bombay *wallah* rainy days.

Down the Grassy Aisles

At the crack of dawn, my dad turns off the cuckoo clock every single day. He chews a piece of antioxidant mint and we set out on the grassy aisle of the suburban Colaba, skirting South Bombay. No talks; just our nods tell the tales. My "hmm's" set the tone for our brief convos as I breathe in his wisdom. We stop at the *chai* stall, drinking our refreshing cups of tea, our chaos blown away by the steam. Our visions turning in a projectile, scanning through the green pastures of the gulf lands, with pools of water and pelicans pecking at every endearing droplet. My Walkman singing Eric Clapton's "My Father's Eyes," and my gaze turns to his eyes, the hazel beauties of creation. Blessed with bonding walks and soulful rendezvous, bound by timelessness, we embrace the dot, dot, dots of life ... one evening he ties my luggage tags and religiously writes my name on them with a black felt pen. We hug each other and bid goodbye. One morning, I open my eyes to the mountains of Massachusetts, waking up to the same cuckoo clock. I think of my dad. I ponder walking down the grassy aisles together. I am brushing away my goose bumps. Because he is gone.

Unique Ambitions

Sitting in a coffee shop, sipping a hazelnut cuppa with just enough cream to dilute the caffeine, eating a sesame bagel caked with jalapeño cream cheese, I am hooked to the sounds of Michael Learns to Rock's "Someday." The melody rings from the wind chimes. Straightening my tangled hair, I look outside to the dancing shades of trees. I draw doodles in the corners of my mind, about the tomorrow of a happening life. Then, it's lunchtime; what's cooking? I gather the ingredients for the South Indian delicacy *arachu vitta sambar*. The mustard seeds begin spluttering, the curry leaves crisping and browning, the herbal essences blend into the cooked lentils. Stumbling upon many questions, the whens and the whys crackle in my mind, the answers wait to roll into the pot...In the morning, curtains are just a wee bit open. I wake up to the sun's rays shrinking my eyes, the glaze brightening a morning smile. There's breakfast in bed and a book by the pot of hazelnut coffee on a tray. It has my name on it.

Tickled in Berkeley

Summer of firsts, this time in Berkeley. En route to the world of medicine, doorways open to the glory of yesteryears, to questions in a research lab. Pipetting solutions, then invading the streets of Berkeley, I am pervaded with the scent of marijuana, skins adorned with tattoos, and free speech in the air. Powered with megabytes of my Discman, I walk the aisles to the Mo'Joe Cafe, sliding into a bumper window seat. An egg-white omelet embellished with cheese and chives waits for my order. Swinging to the beats and singing to the sweet strumming of guitar strings to The Eagles'"Hotel California," I flip through the pages of a sci-fi thriller carrying me to the moon and back. My subtle laughter, the tingling sounds of falling coins, the roar of the crowd when he sings "Welcome to the Hotel California, mirrors on the ceiling and pink champagne on ice." Tickled with glee, my head tilts to the ceiling and sees shiny mirrors melting the impressions of yesterday, today, and tomorrow. The waitress comes by. I pay her my dues and quietly amble out the door, planning for tomorrow, planning for a cure.

I Went to the Bottom of the Well

They hated me, a timid teenager. They bit me with mean dragon fangs, making me weak, shredded from within, stripped of my faith. The dragon's fumes roared at me, turning its neck from side to side. I felt like a trembling half-dead cockroach. Left me feeling like they had shot me in the head, but I bled from down there. After it all, the dragon dove into the water, escaping, extinguishing. I went diving too, to the bottom of the well. There lay a small, shining silver coin. I swam my way through layers of despair, arms as though mustering a breaststroke, and my fingertip reaching out for that coin—my faith. I had found my faith.

Up in the Air

Between sips of an infusion of dry chamomile, I gently stroke my hair. My eyes roll up and down the tiny black-and-white letters of the local newspaper. An advertisement pops up at me. "Will you be my teacher? Will you, please?" The words take me back to my days as a cool teaching assistant in graduate school, marching up and down the pathways of Morrill Science Building with a thick bunch of colored folders, sometimes dropping on the floor, scattering into a rainbow. Then giving a lecture on the sun, the moon, and photosynthesis. There is a synthesis of ideas in my mind, a somersaulting of sorts. I apply for the job, with the cover letter, the curriculum vitae, why I would make a good teacher, and what my students had to say. My mind throws a Frisbee. You gotta throw it to know if it will spin or follow a sad trail and become an awkward *plonk*. So, I threw mine and it's up in the air.

The Passenger Moves On

Clad in green and black, pink pumps with stiletto heels, she barely makes it through her overflowing midsummer night's dream, her unlaundered clothes, the traffic lights, and the low-on-gas car. Her sleepy tones magically vanquishing as her morning cup of coffee beckons. Rummaging through her bag for a credit card, she says, in her sweet voice, to the bubbly barista inhaling the steamy ascend of a cappuccino, moving to Shakira's "Hips Don't Lie." "Oatmeal with cranberries, mixed nuts, and agave syrup; warmed up, please," as though shedding a rhythmic overload of words. "Is that it, ma'am?" He hands the woman an extra packet of sweetness. A verbal rendezvous of sorts, so smooth, so suave, there is no sin, just the synchrony of mellow voices, dipping gestures, heads dropping, and affirmative glances melting the leftover tension from the morning. The time is up, the job is done, love whispers, the train of thoughts rolling its giant wheels, nothing is forbidden anymore. The passenger moves on.

The Dance

The twinkle of hazel eyes, entwining her in the mystery; bronze skin, like a fresh ooze on the palette, curls capturing every bit of swinging romance, a reason to shed the inhibitions and shake the hips, saying *hello!* They dance with ecstatic flow, dousing the unseen reverberations, sparking a glow in the dark. Her lavender skirt twirls and lifts just a bit, exposing her ravishing skin. He bends her in a quintessential dip. Earrings dangle, hearing the secrets in the air, spreading the sweet rapture onto his kind face. The jive comes alive when the sensual bodies of the dancing duo evanesce into a flame.

London Bridge

Descending the driveway in a red Dodge Neon, listening to the Rolling Stones but refusing to be one. He locks a spot in my heart, gently rocks my charming world, until I slumber in love on the hour-long drive. At Detroit International Airport, he excitedly drops the luggage, drops on his knee, holds a velvet green-bowed box that opens to a bejeweled ring. Tiny diamonds and sunshine twinkling out of the box and slipping onto my naked finger. A lip-to-lip entrapment binding the moment that was. He sees me eye to eye, as I childishly pose, his lover becoming a bride-to-be. London calling as the plane touches down at Heathrow Airport. Around Trafalgar Square, water fountains and stone sculptures ride us back to the 16th century. Stepping into the spotlight at Madame Tussauds, we get up close and personal with wax figures of Queen Elizabeth and the Royal Family. We hop on the London Eye, slowly roll on a ferris wheel; oh, my heart trips and strolls on the floor in the company of my beloved. Standing over the London Bridge overlooking the River Thames, we heal the agonies of yesteryears, seal the divisions. We reminisce about the simplicity of a child singing the nursery rhyme. Holding hands, swinging back, then forth, as though through eternal moments of time. Falling in love, we cross the London Bridge.

Sophie

The doorbell rings. I turn the knob, find a brown box with a sunny address label from my friend in Santa Fe. A newborn mom to a newborn child, everyday rides through the tunnels of unknown. Opening the box, ripping wraps, wading my way through the crinkle-cut decorative paper, I find Sophie. Sophie, the spotted giraffe. A small plastic thing, she squeaks when I squeeze her belly. I place it lovingly next to my infant rocking in the cradle. She curls up on the mattress, kicks her feet in the air, and coos away with gaiety. Sophie, her new pet friend. Now and forever.

Infant's Masterpiece

I never thought that our home would be invaded by baby board books, soft plush toys, and rattles, scattered, as though doodles drawn in thin air. Tunes of "Für Elise" and nursery rhymes emerge like a gush of rising clouds from her crib. When baby's eyes twinkle, I hear a mind filled with thunderous wonder. Globes of fond goodness melt within our hearts, tears amble down our cheeks. We ride along this infant's mess, this infant's masterpiece.

Green Bean Mash

Summer celebration in my kitchen. Baby girl wants to cook a culinary paradise with me. We slide a packet full of green beans onto my favorite round and rustic cutting board. She chips the ends; I chop the beans, mixing them with the holy potatoes. What a medley of green and yellow stirring in my pot, stirring my thinking pots. She deftly adjusts her apron straps and turns her chef's cap. We are fellows in the kitchen. She jumps on her toddler stool and reaches out to the microwave and the moon, wanting more. More chores to explore, more doors to open. When the mash stirs, we sweep the corners with a ladle. She dips her spoon in the mash and licks the falling drops, a perfect symphony bubbling in her tiny mouth and in our kitchen.

Sunflowers

A cluster of sunflowers beam on my face. I feel the ever-growing bond. Some yellow, some orange peeking from within, sprouting from their hearts. Now I feel the deluge of love. Suddenly, one flower slants over the green vase, spilling its unseen hues, sprinkling a subtle display of charm. The soft petals look like my little girl's splash of artsy rhythm on a dreamer's canvas. Even the sun shies away from this display of affection, caressing the flowers, whispering, "Oh, dear sunflower, may I join you? May we be one?"

Kindergarten, Here I Come

She kisses me in ecstasy, my dress overflowing the contours of her kind body. She picks her dear daddy's outfit; his red tie matches the red threads of her dress. This year, 2019, she sports her blue graduation cap with dangling strings of sunny yellow. How mellow is the moment when I capture her innocence tumbling into elation. A zygote has turned into a star. Shaking hands, singing the song "Kindergarten, Here I Come" and standing abreast, a statue of pride, holding her diploma curled up into moments of tomorrow. Grinning, marching ahead, her plumes shedding bits of glory. We pick those bits and cry them tears. Boy, isn't she ready to face the world?

The Dry Magnolia Leaves

Oh old, withered leaves of the forlorn magnolia, you lie on a bed under the tree. A lifelong of oily olive, you brighten a passerby's glance. Your debris asks for attention. She cups her little palms and skirts a few, dry leaves, showering them on our oak-wood art table. "Mama let's paint these", then picks a brush, dips it in her favorite yellow and scarlet, and strokes, as though many, many miles. She rounds off in yellow, completing the circle, drawing the sun. The sun shines, the colors blend, the curves and shapes send messages to the world of unknown. Seamless connections flow in a rainbow from violet, indigo, blue, green to the yellow, orange, and red, and the brown and dry magnolia leaves recover and rejoice.

Man Meets Moth

Hiking down the rugged paths of Jordan Lake, I trip on a boulder. The lake, with canoes floating like candles in the wind, just a sight away, blows my thirst and washes my wound. Sporting a pair of yellow Nikes and a yellow dry-wick top, I am Little Miss Sunshine. Long strides through the open, into the woods, reminding me of a maze. I am amazed at the sunlight dancing, nature's reflections gently perching on the wooded trail. My eyes land on an Eastern Tiger Swallowtail, camouflaged on the ground. We match, our yellow stripes, stroking an endless glow of spirits. The synchrony of colors and patterns tells a timeless tale. In this land of opposing forces, man meets moth at the horizon.

I Am Drinking a Cup of Courage

In the middle of stormy seas and monster ripples, a 12-month-old crawls the unseen ladders of fright, a 720-month-old senior is cornered by dementia, a 400-month-old dizzy, staggering mother is ready to drown. Oh God, I cry for a small cup of courage. And God says, "My dear, a cup of courage is not a given, but a birthing." I wander in the wilderness, searching for that enticing cup, gently plucking herbs, shaking and stirring them into the know-it-all of my life. Marrying every rhythm of reality, twisting each misty morning, touching my tummy, I feel the bubbling of something special. Courage is about to be born.

Musings

One December, we meet eye to eye at the coffee shop, at the crooked corner where land meets water. His order is Tall Misto. I had never heard of that drink before. Between sips of coffee and dips of tea, words crisscross, drawing tiny red hearts in my mind's dialog box. Hours pass like tumbling boulders. Picking up my handbag and straightening the crease of my skirt, I say, "Thank you for the coffee!" We hike the mountains of Mackinac Island, sniffing the scent of "Always and forever, you and me" in the air. At the scenic overlooks, we gaze down at the dipping unknown. Shortly after, we quiet the embers of the fireplace in the cabin. With dust-coated ping-pong balls, we play bygone battles, like the ticktock of a pendulum clock with rhythmic rattles. We win, we lose, then suddenly in the air, with a fierce backhand, he smashes and says: "I lost on purpose; I did not want you to feel bad." Little did I know that he lost in the game of ping-pong to win in the name of love.

Red Poppy Flower Peeps

I thought she was gone. But I gave her water, anyway. Every day I made sure she was blessed by the bounty of sunshine and a stream of water trickling from the waterspout to her mouth, refreshing the dry remains of her life, recovering from sadness. The tiny bubbles in line made a soft trail, touching her under the mud, lifting her kindly. I endeared her with pellets of fertilizer and food, her hungry soul, wanting to sprout into glory. I threw in some prayers too; I prayed to the Almighty, "Oh God, she is Mother Nature, bring her back to life, bring her back to me." Today, after a long spell of bathing in love, fondness, and warmth, I saw a red poppy flower peeping into the air, soaring high, then slightly bending to the earth, as though wanting more. She gave me a mouthful of motherly joy. My senses prickled with her blessings, bringing me tears and tearful joys. She told me to keep on going, even if you have tears. She spoke to me in a language only I understood. "Don't cry. The poppies will shine soon, we will be a garden of reddened bliss, so don't think we had to die."

Dancing Tentacles

An hourglass filled with sand, we count the number of times we've erred in life, and the trickling sand, with undue determination, wants more time. We are grown-up kids; we run frantically, fall and wake up with boo-boos on our elbows, in our minds. Dusting off the sand and washing off the wounds, we ask the kid inside us for a bucketful of forgiveness. A reason to throw darts at our souls, for fresh blood to ooze from our hearts, and for our tentacles to dance around in a pool of change.

It Would Be Lovely to Meet You

A writer, there aren't any letters after my name, just the letters that build my words, pop and hop through the keys of my computer, flying, making the sound of a vanishing *swoosh.* I only know when my messages reach you, when you've read them, drawing tiny red hearts and emoji love smiles. Eyelashes blinking slowly as you and I breathe a fresh sigh from our lungs, magically changing our moods. I am in a relationship with you. I sing my poetic tales, you move me through the contours of time, the words spill, we fall in love, and the empathy, ahh…Every once in a while, we muse, adding waves to our hearts, birthing a beautiful writerly bond, counting the beats of joy, the auspices of creation. One such day I will come close to you, singing along, the ebb and flow of my poetic glow. So, come. It would be lovely to meet you.

The Downpour

A roar. A downpour. A dramatic overture. The world outside has shut down. The sky, the swaying, dark trees become darker and darker. For a few moments, seeming like it will be never-say-die, the rowdy rain soon becomes a drizzling poem, collecting in my soft palms, trickling through my fingers. I open my eyes to the world outside. The downpour has settled. Streaks of sun rays kiss the crevices on the tar road. Light appears. Trees become green. Life looks possible from this end of the window.

About the Author

Aruna Gurumurthy is an American author and observer of human nature. Since her childhood in Mumbai, India, she has embarked on a journey of creative exploration and, within her short prose poems, tries to capture the beauty and art in the world. Aruna looks at life with a twinkle in her eyes and a sprinkle on her dreams. From wisdom and discovery to development in *Diya: A Megawatt Approach to Change,* to perceptions and change in *Buddha in The Brain,* and celebration of love, life, and motherhood in *Puppet Dolls* and beyond, Aruna writes on a variety of themes and empowers people from all walks of life. An author of seven books of poetry as well as essays and observations since 2015, Aruna's body of work also appears in the regional anthologies *Heron Clan V* (2018) & *VI* (2019) (Katherine James Books) and the literary journals *FewerThan500* and *What it is to Be A Woman,* reflecting an insightful journey of struggles and jubilations on the path to peace.

Aruna is part of the thriving Southern literary community. She lives with her loving family, including her husband and young daughter, in Chapel Hill, North Carolina.

Kelsay Books

www.ingramcontent.com/pod-product-compliance
Lightning Source LLC
Chambersburg PA
CBHW031154090426
42738CB00008B/1337